Life Evolving
in the
Hands of God

Alan J.F. Fraser

British Library Cataloguing in Publication Data:
a catalogue record for this publication
is available from the British Library

ISBN   978-1-912052-75-2

© **Handsel Press**

The right of Alan Fraser to be identified as the author of this work
has been asserted by him in accordance with
the Copyright, Designs and Patents Act 1988

Unless otherwise indicated, Biblical quotations are from the New Revised
Standard Version of the Bible, copyright © 1989 the Division of Christian
Education of the Churches of Christ in the United States of America

Typeset in 11.5 Minion Pro at Haddington, Scotland

Printed by West Port Print, St Andrews

Introduction

JAMES CLERK MAXWELL
1831–1879

James Clerk Maxwell, viewed by many as the greatest scientist Scotland produced, and often called the father of modern physics, was a sincere Christian. The world-famous Cavendish Laboratory in Cambridge was built for his research. He had had carved above the doors of that prestigious scientific laboratory the Latin Vulgate translation of Psalm 111:2, *Magna opera Domini exquisita in omnes voluntates ejus.* (Great are the works of the Lord, studied by all who delight in them.) That expressed so eloquently how he saw his work as a scientist. On his deathbed he said, "The only desire I can have is like David to serve my own generation by the will of God and then fall asleep." [1 p402, 404]

Centuries before, Johannes Kepler, one of the founders of the modern scientific revolution, wrote, *"Science is the process of thinking God's thoughts after him."* Indeed, there is much evidence to show that modern science grew strongly in the cultural medium of a renewed discovery of Biblical truth.

> "Great are the works of the Lord, studied by all who delight in them." [Psalm 111:2]

Scientists with a Christian faith were predisposed to finding order in the created universe and having confidence in human reason.

Today it is no different. There are still scientists with a strong Christian faith at the forefront of scientific research. Francis Collins, who lead the Human Genome Project (HGP) and served as the director of the US National Institutes of Health during the Covid 19 pandemic, has written a book entitled, "The Language of God". In it he states, *"for me the experience of sequencing the human genome and uncovering this most remarkable of all texts, was both a stunning scientific achievement and an occasion of worship."* [2 p3] In 2018 Dr Jennifer Wiseman, a

Christian astronomer, said, *"I believe science has greatly enriched my faith, by showing me the incredible magnitude, beauty, and activity in the universe, with the largest and smallest imaginable scales of activity intertwined by the laws of physics in intriguing ways."* Quoted in PréCiS (quarterly news from 'Christians in Science'), Spring 2018.

There have been, and still are, many scientists aware of God's hand at work in the course of their scientific research. The exquisite order they are privileged to uncover in the material world reinforces their understanding of creation. The discovery of the laws of nature does not make belief in a Creator redundant but rather reinforces it. Indeed, it gives a reason for their existence. As Alister McGrath says, *"God created the world with an ordered structure, which human beings are able to uncover by virtue of bearing the 'image of God'."* He adds, *"And like it or not, the idea of God remains one of the simplest, most elegant and most satisfying ways of seeing the world."* [3 p79] This is beautifully illustrated in Ruth M. Bancewicz's book, *Wonders of the Living World*. In it the author says, *"Our aim here is simply to showcase the work of six scientists so you can share their sense of wonder and awe, and begin to think about the questions of meaning and purpose that they are asking – including the ultimate question of what this planet is for."* [4 p8]

Three thousand years ago the psalmist said, *"The heavens declare the glory of God, and the firmament proclaims his handiwork."* [Psalm 19:1] Modern science helps us look with wonder at the vast expanses of space and the intricacies of the living cell and the subatomic world, and worship the Creator of it all.

This is not now the most widely accepted view of the relation between science and faith. Dynamic Earth in Edinburgh is, on the whole, an excellent tourist guide to the geological history of the surrounding area. At the start of a journey through time the visitor hears an audible quote from James Hutton, the Glasgow professor who has been called the father of modern geology because of his ground-breaking work explaining the features of the Earth's crust by means of natural processes over geological time. These words spoken by Hutton show his disagreement with a widespread acceptance of Archbishop Usher's dating of creation in the year 4004 BC. However, his words are being used in Dynamic Earth to assert a conflict between the Bible and the findings of geological research. Such a misleading statement is out of place in an educational presentation that puts so much weight on actual evidence and careful reasoning. Mistakenly, there were, and still are, Christians who give credence to such a statement.

There is a similar regrettable confusion among many Christians where 'evolution' is concerned. It is a word that makes some feel uneasy, having grown up with the idea that they must choose between Evolution and the Bible. The more strident voices of atheism assume that Evolution and the Bible are at odds, especially in their understanding of the age of the universe and the origins of the variety of life forms that we know today. The problem lies in their ignorance of the Biblical text and their readiness to use the evidence for the scientific theory of evolution as evidence for 'evolutionism', an atheistic ideology. The confusion is compounded when some Christians also fail to distinguish between evolution and evolutionism.

This book is an attempt to present, in a compact format, the basic evidence, Biblical and scientific, surrounding the idea of life evolving over millions of years. It seeks to demonstrate that both sources of evidence resonate happily to enrich our understanding of origins. It seeks to present the evidence for an evolutionary creation. In doing so I am consciously building on the Calvinist approach to Darwin's ideas, as expressed in the writings of B.B. Warfield of Princeton Seminary (1851–1921), who was quite clear that the Bible was God's authoritative word to human beings, and that it taught nothing against the idea that life had evolved over millions of years. Warfield considered evolution to be a scientific theory that would stand or fall on scientific evidence.

Being a compact presentation, this book cannot give as full a presentation of the evidence as many would prefer. It is kept brief so as to be accessible to a reader with limited time for reading. For a fuller look at the evidence, I would direct the reader to the numbered list of books that have helped me. This is to be found on the final page. References are made to these books throughout the text. The reader is recommended to use them to dig deeper.

The evidence I wish to look at is presented in three sections.

Why It Matters

Truth matters. All truth is God's truth. John Calvin, in his seminal work, "Institutes of the Christian Religion", said, *"If we regard the Spirit of God as the sole fountain of truth, we shall neither reject the truth itself, nor despise it wherever it should appear, unless we wish to dishonour the Spirit of God."*

God speaks to us through creation and through the Bible. Since God is the author of Creation and of the Bible, there can be no conflict between the two. Indeed, the one complements the other and each can shed light on the other. Limited human understanding of the evidence often leads to apparent conflict.

Personal prejudice is a barrier to evangelism. Because of human sin the message of the cross brings its own offence to sinners. That offence can be needlessly increased by tying the Biblical message too closely to fallible human traditions of Biblical interpretation.

Wrong interpretations of Scripture have consequences. Some young people may feel their faith threatened as they come to learn things that brings their inherited interpretations of Scripture into question. Some older Christians may feel a strong loyalty to the tradition they grew up with and feel threatened by the idea of life evolving. This sometimes leads to loss of faith or creates sectarian like animosities that undermine Christian faith and fellowship.

Human interpretations of Scripture are not infallible. God means what he says" is not the same as "God means what I understand him to be saying". It's a question of where the ultimate authority lies. Is the Bible allowed to speak for itself or is it read in the light of received beliefs? When traditional interpretations harden into teaching that cannot be challenged from the Word of God, confusion follows.

Confusion caused by 'evolutionism' v. 'creationism' demands a pastoral response. The church has a pastoral responsibility towards all affected by the confusion between evolutionism, which is an atheistic ideology, and the scientific theory of evolution. Making 'evolution' a no-go area gives credence to the claim of the atheist that evolution disproves the Bible. It encourages the believer to accept the atheist interpretation of the Bible and feel obliged to defend the indefensible.

Ignorance is dangerous. Failure to face up to perceived problems will come back to bite us. Ignorance is never a good defence of the truth. Neither is it a safe option. Being content to live in an apparently secure bubble of shared beliefs, theistic or atheistic, and refusing to engage with the evidence is dishonouring to the God of truth. Bubbles are fragile.

Part 1

Perspective of Scripture

Authority of Scripture

This wee book seeks to take seriously the Biblical text. It is God speaking to us and therefore true in all it affirms. It also recognises that the Bible is a complex book, communicated over many centuries through many authors using many different literary devices and with their varied languages and styles of writing. *"Men and women moved by the Holy Spirit spoke from God"* [2 Peter 1:21].

While the Bible has been written by human authors it is entirely God's word. Paul wrote, *"All scripture is God-breathed . . ."* [2 Timothy 3:16, NIV],[1] and Jesus said, *"The Scripture cannot be broken"* [John 10:35, NIV]. God's revealed word is true and reliable. It is the ultimate authority for all exploration of truth.

> "All scripture is God-breathed . . ." [2 Timothy 3:16, NIV]

However, human understanding of the biblical data is far from infallible, as is human understanding of scientific data.

Misunderstandings on both fronts open up the possibility of an apparent clash between the Bible and science. The problem arises when the Bible seems to say 'X' and Science seems to say 'Y', with 'X' and 'Y' being mutually exclusive. Too often this leads to the rejection of science or the rejection of the Bible, with a reluctance to re-examine the data. With a humbler acknowledgement of human frailty, the apparent clash may be resolved by looking again at the data and discovering that either the Bible does not in fact say 'X', or that science does not really say 'Y', or that 'X' and 'Y' are not actually mutually exclusive.

In both biblical studies and science, new discoveries are made when these questions are faced honestly. Jesus often had to rebuke the experts in biblical studies, the Scribes and the Pharisees, for failing to understand the most important teachings of the Law of Moses, in spite of their vast knowledge of the detail of that Law.

---

1 Copyright © 1973, 1978, 1984, 2011 by Biblica, Inc.; used by permission of Zondervan.

This raises the question of how we get to the truth revealed in Scripture. However, before going on to consider principles of Biblical interpretation we will look briefly at the purpose of Scripture.

Purpose of Scripture

God has spoken to us for a purpose. The Westminster Shorter Catechism (Answer to Question 3) puts it nicely, "The scriptures principally teach what man is to believe concerning God, and what duty God requires of man." In 2 Timothy 3:16 it is important to note the second half of the verse, *". . . and is useful for teaching, for reproof, for correction, and for training in righteousness."* If we wish to know what the Scriptures are saying to us, we need to take into account the purpose for which God's revelation came to us. Scripture speaks clearly in all matters concerning God and our relationship with him. When we want to read between the lines, to see what the Bible implies about historical and material detail we need to take care, lest we read into the Scriptures what the supreme Author never intended to reveal to us.

Sometimes our problem arises when we come to the Bible with the wrong questions. If we seek enlightenment on matters that properly lie in the sphere of science, we need to examine our motives for looking to the Bible for

DONALD M. MACKAY
1922–1987

answers. Are we trying to use the Bible to take a shortcut to scientific truth? Or do we genuinely think we can use Scripture, for God's glory, to oppose the results of scientific research? There is a mixture of motives represented on all sides of the science and faith debate, from arrogance to ignorance, from naïve concern to humble wisdom. Looking for answers to the wrong questions usually leads to confusion rather than enlightenment. We would do well to listen to Donald M. Mackay, a young man from Wick who went on to gain a worldwide reputation for his research into the workings of the brain, and wrote *". . . I want to suggest that the primary function of scientific enquiry in such fields (i.e. relating to the Bible) is neither to verify nor to add to the inspired picture but to help us in eliminating improper ways of reading it."* [5 p151]

At the time of the Reformation some wise and godly men, influenced by the thinking of their age, rejected the Copernican theory because the Bible said, *"You have established the earth and it stands fast."* [Psalm 119:90] Further evidence, confirming the Copernican view, led to a humble rethinking of the traditional understanding of the Biblical text, recognizing that they had formerly read into the Bible what it was not teaching. This willingness to go back to the original texts and to challenge the received teachings of church tradition was characteristic of the Reformation.

> Relating to the Bible ". . . the primary function of scientific enquiry . . . is neither to verify nor to add to the inspired picture but to help us in eliminating improper ways of reading it."
>
> Donald M. Mackay

We recognise that the Bible is a revelation to human beings living in, and part of, a material world. Its narratives do include information on historical or material subjects as part of the mechanism used to reveal God's will to creatures living in space and time. We accept that everything the Bible affirms is true. However, teasing out divine instruction from implied truth about subjects not germane to the main topic of revelation is a dangerous exercise. It is no light matter to hang the authority of God's word on our reading between the lines.

"O send out your light and your truth; let them lead me." [Psalm 43:3]

How to Read the Bible

I remember hearing one minister saying of Genesis 1, "I simply read it as a child would read it." By that he was unconsciously declaring he had no mental baggage that might distort his reading of the Bible, in spite of the fact he had grown up in a particular religious culture, studied in a college that reflected that culture and returned to serve within that culture. Yet he was oblivious to the influence of that culture on his thinking. He was not and still is not alone in thinking this way.

I would suggest five things to bear in mind when reading the Bible:

- the **author's historical context.**
- **our cultural conditioning.**
- the **literary form** of the text.
- the **context of the passage within Scripture.**
- what the passage **tells us about Christ.**

1 Understanding the Author's Historical Context

The Scriptures were written over many centuries to ancient people who lived in a culture far different from our own. It is helpful to remind ourselves that the Bible was not written **to** us, although it was written **for** us. The Bible *"was written for our instruction..."* [Romans 15:4], but if we are to understand what it says we must consider how the original audience would have understood it. Study of other ancient near east literature can be a great help in understanding the cultural baggage of the times and how people in those days communicated truth. Knowing the literary furniture of a bygone age helps us understand a Biblical writer from that age.

> The Bible was not written to us but for us.

John Walton deals with this helpfully in *The Lost World of Genesis One* and *The Lost World of Adam and Eve* [6&7] He looks at other literature from the ancient Near East and gets a feel for the things that were talked about and how they were discussed. His interpretation of Genesis 1 is that it was function orientated. It deals with the creation of function in a cosmos that was "without form and empty". While he believes firmly that the material cosmos was created from nothing by the only living and true God, he believes that Genesis 1 does not teach about material origins. The Hebrew text, seen in its ancient near east context, speaks of six literal days of bringing order into the material world and establishing functions, making it a temple where God would relate to human beings created in his image. [6 p91]

Gordon J Wenham, in his commentary on Genesis, says, *"Genesis 1-11 is a tract for the times, challenging ancient assumptions about the nature of God, the world and mankind."* [8 introduction xlv]

We ought always to ask ourselves what the ancient Israelites would have taken from any OT passage. When we do so we see not only the challenge of God's word to the ancient polytheistic world but also a challenge to the blind adherence to the gods of our own times.

John Calvin, commenting on Genesis 1, said, *"Moses wrote in a popular style things which, without instruction, all ordinary persons, endued with common sense, are able to understand."* [9 p86] Looking for hidden references to modern astrophysics or molecular biology will distort our appreciation of the OT message recorded over 3000 years ago. We should also be prepared to recognise that the ancients had a very different mental picture of the physical universe to the one we have today, informed by space exploration and atomic physics. The mental picture conjured up by the word 'firmament' in the minds of the ancients may well have been that of a solid dome. The Bible neither sets out to promote that view of a flat Earth with a solid dome above nor to correct that view. God's aim was and is to teach what we are to believe concerning God and what duty he requires of us. It has done that very well over millennia, speaking meaningfully to widely varied cultures and levels of understanding of the workings of the material universe.

2 Understanding our own Culture Context

Popular scientific narrative is quite common in our times. We belong to a scientific culture where research into the material world is not only reported in the peer reviewed journals of academia, but also in our newspapers and magazines as well. Living through the Covid 19 pandemic meant that even the least scientifically literate learned something about mutating viruses. Following the scientific advice in a pandemic seemed the right thing to do. We look for explanations in terms of cause and effect in a material world. The scientific narrative of events comes second nature to us. With the mindset of the *The scientific narrative of events comes second nature to us.* modern scientific age, it is too easy to slip into assuming that the early chapters of Genesis are in the form of a simple narrative addressing the chronology of the early days of our universe.

Would the ancient Israelites have viewed it in this way? Our reaction to an ancient message may not be that of those it was originally addressed to. Recognising the existence of cultural biases in our own thinking is essential if we are to let the Biblical text speak to us clearly.

This is particularly important when we go beyond the main themes of a passage and delve into its supposed implications. It reminds me of the join-the-dots puzzles children do. Some bits of the picture are clearly drawn but the rest must be found by joining the numbered dots in the right sequence. By removing dots or adding dots we would end up with a very different picture to that intended. When looking for implied truths in a passage we unconsciously smuggle into the picture ideas influenced by our own culture, these add to the 'dots' we are joining up, and determine the picture we take from the passage

Are we entitled to look to Genesis for answers to questions such as, did God create every plant and animal species separately? Did God really wish to tell us that birds came into being before land animals? Is it important to learn that light and dark, day and night existed before the sun and moon were made? That would be to take our eye of the main story and risk losing our way in the bypaths of implied teaching, looking for answers to questions we have no right to ask of the Biblical text. "I believe what the Bible teaches" is not the same as "The Bible teaches what I believe". What we sincerely believe the Bible teaches may well be a distortion of its real teaching, a distortion caused by looking at the Biblical text through lenses coloured by our cultural formation.

> "I believe what the Bible teaches" is not the same as "The Bible teaches what I believe."

Many centuries ago Augustine of Hippo (354–430 AD) warned in a commentary on Genesis, *"Now it is a disgraceful and dangerous thing for an infidel (unbeliever) to hear a Christian, presumably giving the meaning of Holy Scripture, talking nonsense on those topics (i.e. astronomy etc.) . . . the shame is not so much that an ignorant individual is derided, but that people outside the household of faith think our sacred writers held such opinions, and, to the great loss of those for whose salvation we toil, the writers of our Scriptures are criticised and rejected as unlearned men."* Quoted by Melvin Tinker in *Reclaiming Genesis*. [10 p19]

3 Understanding the Literary Genre

In the writings of the Christian Church from the earliest times it is clear that Genesis 1 was not seen by all as a simple chronological narrative of creation events. Alister McGrath notes, *"Augustine of Hippo (350-430), probably the greatest and most certainly the most influential Christian thinker of that age, taught that, since time was part of the created order, God could not be said to have created the world in time; rather God created the world with time . . . Augustine argued that God brought everything into existence in a single moment of creation."*

[3 p70] Paul Marston appealing to Justin Martyr (c109-165), Clement of Alexandria (c155-220) and Origen (c185-254) as well as a number of Jewish writers concludes, *"the overwhelmingly predominant view of the 'days' amongst both Jewish and Christian commentators in the millennium or so after Christ was that they were neither 24 hour periods nor gave us the 'scientific time order of events'."* [11 p32]

As scientific descriptions of our material world became part of the mental furniture of our culture, it was easy for some Biblical scholars to assume that Genesis 1 was giving a chronology of the early days of the material universe. However, it is clear that was not the uniform understanding of Genesis 1 in the early church, nor did it become established as important to the Christian world view until promoted by Seventh Day Adventists in the 20th Century.

Clearly there is a literary structure that lies on the surface of Genesis 1:1 – 2:4. Although it is not typical Hebrew poetry, it is exalted prose, with its beautiful parallelisms and repetition of words and phrases. The passage starts with the fundamental truth, "In the beginning God created the heavens and the earth", and is followed by God's ongoing development of that created order described in two sets of three days, before ending with the seventh day in which God rests.

- The light of day 1 relates to the luminaries of day 4.

- The sky of day 2 relates to the birds and fish of day 5.

- The land of day 3 relates to the animals and humans of day six.

God's rest on day seven stands on its own. The work of creation is complete.

This literary framework is by no means the only literary device in this passage. David Wilkinson comments, *"Furthermore, the number seven is not just present in the days. For example, the number of Hebrew words in verse 1 is seven. Verse 2 has fourteen. Verses 1 to 3 of Chapter 2 have thirty-five. The word 'God' appears thirty-five times in the chapter, the word 'Earth' twenty-one times, and the phrase 'God saw that it was good' seven times . . .The number seven throughout the Bible is associated with completion, fulfilment and perfection. It speaks of order and goodness."* [12 p24]

Gordon J Wenham in his commentary on Genesis, which lists many other literary devices in Genesis 1:1 – 2:4. [8 pp6ff], says, *"The threefold mention of the seventh day, each time in a sentence of seven Hebrew words, draws attention to the special character of the Sabbath."*

It is also worth noting that the 6+1 literary pattern is prevalent in ancient Near Eastern texts. This was part of the cultural furniture of the ancient Israelites. They would not have been so ready to read this chapter as a simple chronological narrative of material origins. Furthermore, a beautiful literary structure is an aid to memory and facilitates oral communication in an age when few people could read or had access to books. Even in our own age the transcendent beauty of this ancient text made it a fitting passage to read on Christmas eve 1968, as men first orbited the Moon.

> The 6+1 literary pattern is prevalent in ancient Near Eastern texts. This was part of the cultural furniture of the Israelites.

A comparison between the first and last books of the Bible is not unreasonable. In both, the number seven figures prominently. In our culture numbers are simply numbers, although when talking of dozens or thousands we may use numbers more loosely. In the ancient near east numbers had qualitative as well as quantitative significance. This, too, should make us cautious when interpreting this ancient text.

In both Genesis and Revelation there are two realms interacting closely – the heavenly realm and the earthly realm, the realm where God dwells and the realm where we live out our time on planet Earth. The first deals with God bringing into existence an orderly framework of time and space and all that they encompass for us as material/spiritual beings. The latter deals with a war in the heavenly realm with many of the battles being fought out in our time and space, with the promise of a new or renewed creation which will complete the work began at the dawn of time. In both, figurative language should be expected.

The literary structure approach to Genesis 1 was promoted over the twentieth century by Biblical scholars of unquestionable competence and integrity who had the highest respect for the Scriptures. This can be followed up in Henri Blocher's *In the Beginning* [13 pp49ff] and in an article entitled 'Space and Time in the Genesis Cosmogony' Meredith G. Kline, a professor at Westminster Seminary, U.S.A. The great merit of this approach is that it treats the text with respect.

Kline says, "This is heavenly time, not earth time, not time measured by astronomical signs . . . the unending nature of the seventh day of creation differentiates it from earthly, solar days." Hebrews 4:4,9,10 enjoins God's people to look forward to the Sabbath rest that lies ahead for them. The six days of divine work followed by a seventh day of rest is part of God's gracious provision for those made in his image. Walton says that after the work of the six days God entered the control room of the cosmos to maintain the order created.

For Kline, "The creation week is to be understood figuratively, not literally. That is the conclusion demanded by the Biblical evidence." For Walton the creation week is a literal week but has nothing to do with material origins but with the creation of a functional order. One thing is clear, we should think carefully before reading this revelation, given to an ancient near east people, as a simple narrative of material origins, like a popular scientific account of cosmogony.

> "The creation week is to be understood figuratively, not literally." Kline

4 *Understanding the Biblical Context*

The fourth rule for understanding a Biblical passage is to see how it relates to the rest of Scripture. The first chapters of Genesis give vital information about God and humans that form the bedrock on which God's revelation to humans is built. The Bible starts with creation and ends with the new creation. It unfolds the divine plan for those created in his image and likeness, developing his plan for the redemption of sinful human beings, created for communion with the Almighty and holy God, estranged by their sin and brought into relation with God himself, as

> The first chapters of Genesis form the bedrock on which God's revelation to humans is built.

sons and daughters for whom a place has been prepared in the new creation, the goal of God's creation plan.

Teaching on creation pervades the whole of Scripture. God is seen as not just the remote Creator but the ever-present Sustainer of all that exists. In a few places there are some references to the creation story in Genesis. We will look at some of them below. It should be noted at this point that what the authors themselves thought about cosmology was limited by their human understanding. What they taught was divinely inspired. When the psalmist said, "*. . . the earth . . . stands fast*", he was not necessarily conscious of using metaphorical language. He might well have believed that the earth was flat and static as he wrote, but his words, under divine guidance, did not teach that ancient picture of the world. Cosmology was not what the Psalmist was teaching.

Those who disagree with this position often turn to the following four Biblical texts to prove their assertion that Genesis does teach cosmology.

Exodus 20:11 "*For in six days the Lord made heaven and earth, the sea, and all that is in them, and rested the seventh day; therefore, the Lord blessed the Sabbath day and consecrated it.*" This, on the face of it, seems to endorse the 6x24 hour creation belief. Two things should be noted. First, it is dangerous to hang so much inferred teaching on the apparent implications of a text that sets out to teach us where our ultimate identity and security lies, and to mandate a weekly remembrance of God and his provision for us. Second, as far as our interpretation of the 'days' is concerned, this text adds nothing to the text of Genesis 1. The interpretations of Kline or of Walton remain valid options.

Matthew 19:4 "*Have you not read that the one who made them at the beginning 'made them male and female'.*" Jesus' teaching is based on a recognition of the authority of Genesis and its teaching about the nature of human beings, as they relate to one another, especially in marriage. It says nothing about chronology other than that male and female existed from the beginning.

Acts 17:26 "*From one ancestor he made all nations to inhabit the whole earth.*" Once again it is dangerous to build a case for the theory that every human being that ever existed was descended physically from Adam, on the apparent implications of Paul's words to the philosophers at Athens. Paul may well have believed such a view of human origins. We simply cannot know what his private thoughts were on this point, but we should note that his words to the Athenians, recoded in Scripture, do not explicitly teach that belief.

Romans 5:12 "*. . . and death came through sin, and so death spread to all because all have sinned.*" Paul speaks of the transmission of sin throughout the human race. Adam has clearly some representative status. Physical descent from Adam is not mentioned and need not be implied. There may well have been other living beings with a similar human genome contemporary with Adam who was the first to be endowed with a spiritual nature and brought into a personal relationship with his Maker – the first to be a truly human being in the Biblical sense, the first to be created in the image of God. The historical existence of Adam and Eve is consistent with the idea that life, including human life, evolved. The idea that Adam's material nature had come about through God's guiding the evolution of living beings in no way undermines Paul's teaching.

5 Asking How the Passage Grows our Understanding of Christ

The focal point of Scripture is the birth, death and resurrection of Jesus. What comes before and what comes after is to be interpreted in the light of these pivotal events. In Genesis the stage is set for the amazing story of God's working out his redemptive plan. What God began in Genesis he will complete in the new heavens and the new earth. Christ's resurrection is the guarantee of the resurrection of all the redeemed. The entrance of sin into the world is finally dealt with in the new creation where sin is banished for ever, all being the outcome of a plan that existed from before the creation of the world. The Creator's walking with humans in the garden of Eden is to be fully realised in the new creation where *the home of God is among mortals . . . he will wipe every tear from their eyes. Death will be no more.* [Rev 21:3,4] Human beings made in the image of God will finally realise their divinely ordained destiny, giving glory to God forever, praising God not only for the wonder of his creation but also for the even greater wonder of his redemptive love, exploring for all eternity the infinite riches of the one who made them and who died for them.

> The focal point of Scripture is the death and resurrection of Jesus.

To appreciate this story, an understanding of the first chapters of Genesis is vital. A very readable introduction is found in Alasdair Paine's book, *The First Chapters of Everything* (14).

Some basic teachings in Genesis 1 to 3

1 God

God is. *"In the beginning God created . . ."* [Genesis 1:1, NIV] The Bible simply starts with the eternal, uncreated God bringing into being everything else that exists – time, space, matter, spiritual beings. He is the starting point for our understanding of everything else.

God alone is to be worshipped. The Sun and Moon, worshipped by the nations surrounding Israel, are things that God made.

God created through his word and by his Spirit. He commanded and things came into being. Without him nothing was made that has been made

God is something other than the world he brought into existence. He did not convert some part of himself into physical energy and matter, nor is he the rational soul of the material universe.

Genesis 1 is consistent with the fundamental Biblical truth that **God created from nothing.** God alone is eternal. While the word *'bara'* does not always mean creation from nothing (*ex nihilo*) it is certainly the most suitable word to use for such divine activity.

Much of Genesis 1 tells how **God acted sovereignly through the created order.** *"Let the Earth put forth vegetation . . ."* [1:11] and *"Let the waters bring forth with swarms of living creatures . . ."* [1:20] are indications that the Creator was active in the physical processes he had brought into being.

In Genesis 1 there is a strong emphasis on **God bringing order into his creation.** God 'separated' things or 'made' things, thus putting order rather than substance into his creation, so that it would no longer be 'without form and void'.

God is the ultimate authority in the universe. The creation belongs to him. Any abuse of the natural world is an attack on the Creator.

God is not a dumb spiritual force (not 'The Force' as in Star Wars nor the impersonal entity Einstein believed in) nor dumb like the idols of the nations around Israel. When Israel's God speaks things happen.

God is personal. *"Let us make humankind in our image . . ."* In Genesis 2 God relates in a personal way with Adam and Eve. He talks with them and listens to them. He provides for them food and meets their emotional needs. The 'us' may also be a hint that this God is a plurality of persons but one God.

2   Human Beings

The word '**create** (*bara*) occurs in only three places in Genesis 1. The first time in v1 deals with the creation of the heavens and the earth. The second time in v21 deals with the creation of life in the sea and in the air. Then in v27 the word is dealing with the creation of human beings. There is something particularly significant in the creation of human beings. By day 6 the dust of the Earth was already there. Animal life was already there, but with human life there was something new, something more than mere matter.

On the day God created human beings he had also made land creatures. We are reminded that we have something in common with the inanimate world of matter and even more with the animals. This is a good reason for respecting God's creation. We are part of it.

God formed human beings 'dust from the earth' – a literal rendering of the original Hebrew text and the ancient Greek translation of that text (the Septuagint). The text says nothing of the mechanisms or techniques God used when going from inanimate matter to a living human being. Did God make a figure from 'dust' or fashion the first man from clay like a potter and then turn it into a living being, or did he use a long process **of his own design**, ending up with a hominid into which he breathed the quality necessary for it to become a person made in His own image? Perhaps the lack of detail is meant to discourage us from trying to find answers in the Bible to the trivia that intrigue us, rather than focussing on the truths God wants us to hear.

Human beings relate to God in a personal manner. God said, *"Let us make humankind . . ."* The creation of humans was a personal thing with God. In creating human beings God, who is love and who existed from all eternity in a perfect relationship of love, brought into being creatures made in his own image and likeness. God entered into a living, personal relationship with human beings. The picture of him walking in the garden in the cool of the day is a beautiful little cameo of a loving relationship. We might even think of God looking forward to this evening stroll and Adam finding this the highlight of his day. Fellowship with God is of the essence of human life and always will be.

Human beings relate to one another in a personal manner. This characterises human beings. God made them male and female. He created diversity and plurality within humankind, a diversity and plurality that enabled man to exercise love in a deep personal relationship. "*It is not good that the man should be alone.*" [Gen 3:18] Adam searched among the animals for a soulmate and could not find one. In Eve God provided one of whom Adam could say, "*This at last is bone of my bones and flesh of my flesh.*" She was taken from Adam's side (the Hebrew word often translated here as 'rib' is nowhere else in the Bible used in an anatomical sense. It tends to be used architecturally denoting one side or another). Perhaps we are to understand that Eve was Adam's other half. Together they formed a new entity, a two in one that reflects something of the three in one of the Creator. Both male and female were equal in God's eyes, both made in the image of God. Within the full range of enriching personal relationships that would develop as the human community grew, that of marriage would lead to the family and a further expansion of mutual loving relationships.

Human beings have a moral faculty, an essential quality if they are to have fruitful contact with a holy God. Adam and Eve were given the challenge of obeying or disobeying God. They clearly understood the difference between right and wrong. They chose to disobey with far reaching consequences for the whole human race and beyond.

Adam was God's representative on Earth. He was given a role in Eden to guard it and to cultivate it. Genesis 2 gives no hint of what the world was like outside the garden. Whatever it was like it was created 'good' or 'fit for purpose', a description that does not exclude the existence of carnivorous animals keeping the herbivore population in balance.

The picture of the human relationship to God in Genesis is far removed from the accounts of creation of the ancient contemporaries of Israel, who have man created to provide food for the gods. God does not need a human being to feed him, rather he provides for humans in all their needs. As the rest of Scripture unfolds, we see an ever more wonderful picture of God's unceasing provision, including redemption through Christ, and ending with the hope of eternal communion with God in the new heavens and the new earth 'wherein dwells righteousness'. What we see in Genesis is the beginning of a work of creation that will be fully consummated in our eternal life as resurrected beings.

3 The Non-human World

Our space time universe had a beginning. The first words of Genesis, *"In the beginning God created the heavens and the earth"*, assume a beginning. The idea of 'Creation out of nothing' (*creatio ex nihilo*) certainly resonates well with Genesis 1 and fits New Testament teaching. It undermines pagan ideas of an eternal universe.

God not only created but remains active in the universe. In every part of the creation story the emphasis is on God as the One who brought all things into existence and continues to be active in the created processes of the material world. Even time itself was created by the eternal God, who lives outside of our time frame but interacts with us in our time frame. The author of the letter to the Hebrews speaks of him as the one *"through whom he also created the worlds . . . and he sustains all things by his powerful word."* [Hebrews 1:2,3]

The whole world is God's creation and so has great value. The phrase *"And God saw that it was good"*, i.e. fit for purpose, is repeated seven times in Genesis 1. This has implications for the way we treat the nonhuman world. It has value and must be respected. To destroy God's good creation is an act of vandalism that will have serious consequences for the world and for our relationship to its creator.

The created world is orderly. The mention of *"plants yielding seed of every kind . . ."* [v12], *"the great sea monsters and every living creature that moves of every kind"* [v21], and *". . . cattle and creeping things and wild animals of the earth of every kind"* [v24], presents a picture of an ordered world. There is nothing capricious about the creator's work. He works in creation and in providence in an orderly manner. The identification of 'kinds' with any modern scientific classification is quite gratuitous. It would have been meaningless to the original recipients of this revelation.

Such order, along with man being made in the image of God, is a sound basis for scientific research. Early Christian scientists saw this order not as the order of a manufactured clockwork machine but rather as the orderly thinking of the Creator who sustains the universe moment by moment. This thorough going theism is congruent with Scriptural accounts of Jesus turning water into wine, stilling a storm, giving sight to one born blind or raising Lazarus from the dead. Miracles have impact when seen against our normal daily experience of an ordered world.

There is no indication of how long God took to bring the universe from its beginning to the point where human beings walked the earth. Neither does it teach us that seed-bearing plants existed before sea creatures were created. It does not even imply that there were fruit trees before birds. Science is the God-given discipline for determining how old the universe is. It's not a question the author of Scripture has set out to answer. Why would he? There were far more important things all human beings needed to know. It is, however, interesting to note that the idea of a beginning resonates well with scientific evidence.

Within the text of Genesis 1 and 2, there are indications that a simple narrative of material origins in six consecutive twenty-four-hour days was not intended.

While light is called into existence in Day 1 the sun and moon are made (not simply appeared) on Day 4.

Chapter 2 verse 5 presupposes the normal relationship between rain and plant growth and speaks of a period without bush or small plants. It is difficult to fit such a scenario into a literalistic interpretation of dry land appearing on Day 3 with vegetation.

Adam, in Chapter 2, is recorded as having had time to name all the animals and fail to discover any among them that could relieve a sense of being alone. Eve is then formed and brought to Adam. Chapter 1 talks of human beings, male and female being created on Day 6.

It would be crass arrogance to see these as indications of errors by ignorant ancient people. The whole passage is so well constructed it was clearly not the work of ignorant people. It is better to recognise that the passage was never intended to be read as a divinely accredited chronology of physical events.

Some other approaches to the Genesis records note that ancient Hebrew manuscripts were written with no punctuation. Modern translations have to provide capital letters, full stops etc. This has given rise to the following suggestions for harmonizing the text of Genesis 1 with modern science.

By using parenthesis in the accounts of the six days it is possible to read these accounts with the opening and closing words of each 'day' to refer to creative commands, the rest of the verses pertaining to that 'day' being seen as a literary parenthesis which refers to activity over a long period of time. This allows the 'evening and the morning' to be taken literally whilst still allowing time for development in the long ages following each day.

A variation in the punctuation of the first verses can allow for a gap of indefinite length between the beginning of verse 1 and the later six days of creation. This was popular among some in the 19th century but has long faded from view as it merely allows for a great age for the universe but does not accommodate the epochal development of planet Earth.

Finally, legitimate punctuation could see the six twenty-four-hour days as periods in which God revealed to Adam how he had created the world. The periods of God's actual activity in creation and development would be separate from these days of revelation.

None of these suggestions sits well with our knowledge of the ancient culture of the original authors and their target audience. Nor does it sit comfortably with our scientific knowledge of geological processes, biological development over long ages and our understanding of the human genome.

Appreciating the First Chapters of Genesis

The first chapters of Genesis are often seen as an embarrassment for the educated Christian of the 21st century. The agnostic certainly believes they are out of step with the accumulated evidence of science. However, if read with an open mind and a willingness to hear what God wants to say to us, then they are among the most sublime passages in all literature. God is communicating to a huge variety of people groups, in many centuries and with varied cultures, timeless truths that are vital for our eternal welfare. When we spend our time with this passage on issues tangential to the main thrust of the passage, we are in danger of mishandling a precious gift from God. The ancient Hebrew account of creation lacks all the gross features of their pagan contemporary accounts with all their warring gods and goddesses. It was probably read by the contemporaries of Moses with reference to their perceived understanding of the physical world, possibly even with a solid firmament covering a flat Earth and with waters stored above that firmament. However, it strikingly refrains from promoting that ancient cosmology. It refrains from teaching a three-decker view of the universe, or any other cosmology for that matter.

The teaching in Genesis and the teaching of science are complementary. They look at different aspects of the truth. Their different perspectives come up with important truths that are in no way contradictory. A page of a book may be studied scientifically by measurement of page dimensions, paper tint, chemical properties of ink, etc. Such a description would be accurate and would in no way contradict the viewpoint of the reader who finds the paper and ink conveys a message of great importance. So it is with the Biblical account of origins and the description of a developing universe according to cosmology and biological evolution. The Bible deals with ultimate origins. Science deals with existing material reality, dealing with the functioning of what is there, but unable to explain why there is something there rather than nothing at all. As an account of where we've come from, Genesis is awesome in its capacity to reach so many people across so many cultures, with such a wide range of intellectual ability.

The teaching of Genesis and the teaching of science are complementary.

> Worthy are you our Lord and God,
> To receive glory and honour and power,
> For you created all things,
> And by your will they existed and were created.
>
> [Revelation 4:11]

Part 2

Perspective of Science

Why Science Matters

Science seeks to make sense of the material world using reason, observation, measurement and not a little creative imagination.

It is no accident that the modern scientific revolution took place when men were rediscovering the teaching of Scripture, being encouraged by the Reformers to go back to the original data and think for themselves, thus producing not only great Biblical scholars and theologians but also great scientists, (e.g. Bacon, Boyle, Galileo). Galileo is often portrayed as being at odds with Biblical teaching. Far from it. He was at loggerheads with the authorities in his church because of their reading of Scripture through the lens of Aristotelian philosophy. This had dominated the minds of philosophers and theologians for more than a thousand years. Because the Creator has revealed himself to us and has made us in his own image, we are confident that the material world is orderly and that that order can be legitimately and usefully investigated by us. Albert Einstein once said, *"The most incomprehensible thing about the universe is that it is comprehensible."* (Quoted by Alister McGrath in *Inventing the Universe.* [3 p76]

The atheist often declares that science has made redundant any need for belief in God. Quite the contrary is true. Theism provides a solid basis for doing science. Theism faces the big questions of origins, truth, purpose and reason.

> "The most incomprehensible thing about the universe is that it is comprehensible." Albert Einstein

How Science Operates

It is the normal practice of scientists to try to make sense of the material world through observing, then postulating, testing and refining theories. The Greek root of the word 'theory' has to do with seeing. A theory is "a way of seeing things". [3 p21] It is not a vague phase between hypothesis, seen as an inspired guess, and confirmed natural law, but an as yet incomplete view of reality. (We may see systematic theology in a similar light. The varied theologies are imperfect ways of seeing the Biblical text. Biblical research and theological debate help to move towards a better understanding of revealed truth.)

Scientific theories change over time as new evidence arises. Indeed, a mark of a strong theory is that it not only explains what we already know but also helps uncover new evidence, being capable of modification in the light of that evidence. The Flat Earth theory seemed common sense to people going about their daily rounds, but more careful observation of ships at sea and celestial bodies suggested a spherical Earth. (Eratosthenes, around 250 BC actually measured the circumference of the Earth, coming up with an answer fairly close to what we know today! However, it took many centuries for this to become generally accepted.) In 1543 Copernicus challenged the prevailing view that the Earth was the centre of the universe. He suggested that the Earth and other planets revolved round the sun in circular orbits. When Kepler observed not circular but elliptical orbits the Copernican model itself was refined. The 'Steady State' theory, much in vogue last century especially among atheists, was dropped in favour of the 'Big Bang' theory in the light of further evidence.

Science progresses in this way. Scientists make their reputations by improving on existing theories, by paying attention to the evidence. All theories are provisional, subject to modification in the light of further evidence. Some theories may be rejected in their entirety. Most are strengthened by further evidence while continuing research into what is yet unexplained. In the providence of God, people made in his image continue to progress in their understanding of the material world through the powerful tools of scientific research. To God be the glory.

I like to think of the scientist tackling a vast jigsaw, where the number of pieces is unknown and there is no picture on the box. Science has filled in parts of the picture but much more awaits assembly. Where science is working fruitfully in a particular area an image of reality begins to emerge. Long before all the pieces are in place, or even where a few are mistakenly placed, a picture emerges. It becomes clear what material reality looks like in that area. Theories may come and go, or more often be modified in the light of new evidence, but the view we have of the material universe grows in clarity. I speak of material reality because that is the sphere of operation of the natural sciences. There are other spheres, interrelating with one another, that deal with the big questions of truth, reason, ethics, aesthetics, spiritual beings, meaning, personal identity, love etc. These require other tools to explore them.

World of Inanimate Matter

The Age of the Universe

The Big Bang Theory basically paints a picture of an incredibly dense universe of energy and space expanding rapidly, with energy converting

into Hydrogen atoms which collect under gravity forming stars. In the centre of these stars nuclear fusion converted Hydrogen into Helium and then on to building all the other elements. Mature stars exploded, in what is called a super nova, sending matter into the wider universe. From this all the stars and planets are formed. Even we are formed from 'star dust'. It took 13.8 billion years for this process to take place, with our own planet Earth being around for 4.5 billion years.

The evidence for this theory has grown over the past century. The Big Bang Theory predicted the existence of a faint background radiation originating from the processes involved in the earliest moments of the existence of the universe. That background radiation has been discovered and measured and is in agreement with the theoretical predictions. Its consistency with a mathematical ordering of the material world is impressive.

Observations of immense gas clouds, exploding stars, measurements of the rate of expansion of the universe (using the Doppler Effect), etc., all add to this impressive confirmation of the theory. The time it takes for light to travel from the most distant stars and galaxies requires the universe to have been in existence for many billions of years.

To many Christians the Big Bang theory cries out for a theistic approach to the universe. It points to the majesty, wisdom and power of the Creator. The enormous forces involved, the exquisite balance, the precise timing of events, the mathematical precision of it all and the sheer beauty of the universe out there leads us to a new appreciation of the words of the psalmist, *"The heavens are telling the glory of God."* [Psalm 19:1]

Age of Planet Earth

The age of the Earth has been computed from a variety of areas of observation, all coming together in impressively close agreement. These areas of measurement include:

- Radioactive decay of elements. (When this was applied to a number of meteorites, unaffected by Earthly geological processed the result was a remarkably consistent dating for them all of close to 4.55 billion years.)

- Build-up of sediment on ocean floors and subsequent conversion under pressure into sedimentary rock.

- Cooling of molten lava and formation of igneous rock.

- Metamorphic rock with its initial formation under pressure being followed by extreme heat in the depths of the Earth followed by subsequent exposure and weathering.

- Rock of a sedimentary type with intrusions of igneous material.

- Ice core samples from Antarctica go back 720,000 years.

- Tectonic plate movement and its implications for the basic structure of the surface of our planet. The rate of movement of the plates on either side of the Atlantic Ocean can be measured today. The geological evidence from both sides and the shape of the continents on both sides, with the continuing appearance of volcanic islands near Iceland, all confirm the theory of continental drift.

> Evidence from widely varied disciplines converge on an age for planet Earth of 4.5 billion years.

It is truly remarkable that the immense weight of evidence, from widely varied disciplines, converge on an age for planet Earth of 4.5 billion years.

World of Living Things

The 19th century gave us a new way of looking at the world of living things. Charles Darwin promoted the emerging theory of evolution and added his own idea of Natural Selection, a process akin to animal breeding but driven by natural forces. Initial reaction from the scientific establishment was divided. As with many bold new theories the idea was attractive but the evidence initially sparse. Since then, the evidence has mounted up impressively for the view that life has evolved from simple beginnings over many millions of years to produce the diversity we know today.

Scientific Evidence for Evolution

The initial evidence for Evolution, what Darwin called "descent with modification", came from a study of life forms in different parts of the world widely separated from each other. This has been greatly strengthened by evidence from genetics, molecular Biology and the study of genomes.

1 Comparative Anatomy. The earliest evidence for common descent came from studying living organisms, noting how isolated parts of the world contained different kinds of animals, birds and reptiles that were similar to those known in Europe. There are old world monkeys and new world monkeys. There are Southern Hemisphere marsupials that parallel Northern Hemisphere mammals. It looked as if all belong to a family tree, descended from common ancestors but developing along separate lines in tune with the different conditions prevailing in their separate environments.

Later anatomical studies produced further evidence to support this idea. Some beetles have perfectly formed wings trapped beneath a hard outer shell. Most pythons have a pelvis like that of animals with legs. These features are easily explained as resulting from a development process where ancestors with these features passed them on to descendants that ceased to need them.

2 Fossil Evidence. The increasing discovery of fossils, the record in rock of ancient life forms, gives a remarkable picture of life developing from simpler to more complex forms over the ages spanned by the rocks in which they are found. Determine the age of the rock and you know the age of the fossil. This pattern of simpler life forms in older rocks graduating to more complex life forms in later rocks is observed across the planet. Nothing but the remnants of bacteria are found in rocks older than 1.5 billion years. Between 500 and 570 million years ago there appears to have been a relatively rapid development of the body plans that are found in varied animal life today. This is referred to as the Cambrian explosion. Later there appeared amphibians and insects, then reptiles then mammals. Nowhere on our planet do you find rock strata with reptiles before the first appearance of amphibians, nor amphibians before the first appearance of fish.

It is also interesting to note that the first amphibians to appear have more fish like characteristics than later amphibians; the first reptiles appear to have more amphibian features and the first mammals more reptilian features. Basilosaurus, a fossil whale, retains a complete mammalian hind limb which would have been buried beneath layers of blubber, evidence that whales were descended from land mammals. Many of the fossils are records of life forms that have not survived, e.g. dinosaurs. Within this pageant there are life forms that appear to be transitional between one species and another.

> Fossils tell a consistent story over billions of years

Denis Alexander records the account of an expedition of palaeontologists to Greenland that went home with a good number of fossils. Some of these fossils appeared to show development from true fish to land animals. However, there was a gap in the series, so they went back again and concentrated on the rock strata that should contain the missing member of the series. They found it, the Tiktalik, with just the characteristics it should have and in strata of the right age. [15 p128]

Fossils tell a consistent story of increasing complexity of life forms over billions of years.

Million years ago	Era	Period	
65	Cenozoic	Quaternary + Tertiary	
145	Mesozoic	Cretaceous	First primates First flowering plants
199		Jurassic	First birds
251		Triassic	First mammals First dinosaurs
299	Paleozoic	Permian	
359		Carboniferous	First reptiles First trees
416		Devonian	First amphibians
444		Silurian	First vascular plants
488		Ordovician	
542		Cambrian	First fish First animals with backbone
2500	Precambrian	Proterozoic	Simple life in seas
4000		Archean	Earth's crust forms
4600		Hadean	Planet Earth forms

GEOLOGICAL AGES

3 The Genome. The development of the science of genetics helped explain how Natural Selection works, especially how new characteristics in living organisms could arise through mutation and hybridisation. Each plant or animal cell has a nucleus with chromosomes which consist of long strands of DNA. These are passed from one generation to the next and contain the recipe for the formation of each individual. Further work on DNA in living cells increasingly shows the enormous impact of even tiny changes to the DNA, causing significant changes to the physical and mental existence of living organisms.

Today we hear a lot about the Genome. It has been possible to determine the actual molecular structure of the chromosomes and so see the precise molecular code that seems to define the characteristics of the individual. This is known as sequencing the Genome. The official body responsible for the Human Genome Project was headed by Francis S. Collins, a scientist with strong Christian convictions. He wrote a book called *The Language of God*. [2] The Genome Project has provided a new line of evidence for evolution, quite separate from, but highly supportive of, the older evidence from the fossil record. There are clear similarities at the molecular level across the whole animal kingdom. There is also clear evidence for increasing complexity and thus evidence for common descent from ancient living creatures. In our material nature we, human beings, are part of this whole process. The human genome reads as if the human material constitution is a development of that of ancestral species.

The fossils and the Gnome seem to be singing from the same hymn sheet.

Fossil evidence of Hominids and 60,000-year-old cave art further strengthen the belief that human-like beings have been around for possibly as much as 250,000 years.

From two very different sources, from fossils and from the Genome, comes the same powerful message. Life has existed for millions of years, existing initially in simpler forms and gradually developing into the full gamut of all the complex and varied species we know today. The fossils and the Gnome seem to be singing from the same hymn sheet.

Perhaps the most difficult challenge for theists came from the attempt to explain this evolutionary development of living beings through natural forces which are seen to operate through random events. This seems to remove God from the world of living things as previous generations thought he had been removed from the physical world of matter and energy. We will look at that in Part 3.

There was a time when the movements of the planets were considered to be the direct action of God as distinct from the day-to-day workings of the world around us. As these planetary orbits were explained in the heliocentric view of Copernicus and Kepler there seemed less place for divine action. Perhaps God was only directly involved in the movement of the comets or the peculiar 'retrograde' movements of Mars. But these movements were later shown to be explicable in terms of physical forces acting on material bodies. Then it was thought that organic matter was somehow different from inorganic matter. But that too was shown to be incorrect. And so the 'god of the gaps' became smaller and smaller.

However, there were others who rejoiced in every new discovery of God's order in the material world. They saw, not a god that attended to the bits we cannot explain, but the God who is responsible for bringing all things into being and continuing to sustain their existence in a beautiful, ordered, creation.

Part3

How Christians Reacted

In the Theory of Evolution, aimed at explaining the diversity of existing life forms, there are three strands which gave rise to debate within the Church.

1 The Earth is very old.

2 All existing life forms have developed from single-celled organisms.

3 The evolutionary process is driven by Natural Selection working on random mutations in the DNA of living organisms.

From the start Christians were divided, with some welcoming the new ideas and others condemning them as undermining confidence in biblical teaching. Atheists latched onto the latter reaction and claimed that the Bible had been discredited in its teaching on origins and could no longer be trusted on anything it taught. This weaponizing of the Theory of Evolution caused some Christians to react against the idea of life evolving.

1 The age of the Earth was calculated by Archbishop Usher attempting to use data from the Bible. He dated creation in the year 4004 BC. Early in the 20th century the Seventh Day Adventists took a strong line insisting on creation in six twenty-four-hour days less than 10,000 years ago. Later this was picked up by some conservative Christians in the USA and has its zealous following today. Among Biblical scholars from the Reformed school there was a greater readiness to question this young earth interpretation. Light shed by science on the age of the Earth prompted Christians to rethink their previous interpretation of Scripture, not as a craven attempt to align Scripture with current scientific theories, but as a humble recognition of the need to look again at the Biblical data and consider whether or not they had been misinterpreting it. All truth is God's truth and helpful in making us aware of our prejudices.

Scotland was at the forefront of the geological revolution of the 19th century and among the big names were not only agnostics but also strong Christians such as Hugh Miller, a stone mason from Cromarty, who built up an international reputation for careful geological observation and an engaging literary style. He was inclined to see the

Hugh Miller 1802 – 1856
here depicted by artist D.O. Hill
at the Disruption Assembly of 1843

days of Genesis as long ages, so as to reconcile the Genesis account with the evidence of the rocks. That the Earth was around for a long time, millions or billions of years, was also generally accepted by the founding fathers of the Free Church of Scotland, including Thomas Chalmers who proposed the reconstruction theory that suggested Genesis 1:1 recorded God's initial creation which was followed after an indefinite time by a lapse into chaos. The rest of Genesis 1 was then taken to be an account of the creation reconstructed. [13 p41] One way or another there was widespread belief, among leading conservative thinkers, including Charles Hodge, A. A. Hodge, B. B. Warfield and C. H. Spurgeon, that the universe had an ancient history.

In the twenty-first century there are many Christian scientists working at the cutting edge of their disciplines, faithful to God and faithful to science, humbly seeking truth in God's creation and using their God given faculties. Among them are geologists who see no tension between their faith and their scientific research that proves, beyond all reasonable doubt, that Planet Earth has been around for over four billion years.

Carol Hill is a geologist with over forty years of research in the Grand Canyon of Arizona, USA. In her book, *A Worldview Approach to Science and Scripture*, she provides a thoughtful and beautifully presented analysis of the Biblical and scientific evidence for the age of the Earth. Her research in the Grand Canyon presents a picture of dark Precambrian rock covered by successive layers of Palaeozoic sedimentary rock with Mesozoic on top of that. The rock types include metamorphic (formed under immense heat and pressure), igneous (formed from volcanic activity) and sedimentary (formed by sediment settling at the bottom of an ocean and producing limestone and sandstone rocks from an original variety of ecosystems). [16 p100] This picture of rock formed over billions of years is enriched by discoveries of periods of rock erosion followed by further sedimentation, of ripple marks and ancient soils. It is hardly surprising that Carol Hill cannot subscribe to the idea that a global flood created the Grand Canyon in less than one year.

However, Carol Hill does believe that the account of Noah's ark represents an historical event. She argues that this account tells the story of a massive flood in the area of modern Iraq. She tellingly notes that the concept of Planet Earth would have been quite foreign to the people of Moses' day and earlier. A story of a global flood would have been unintelligible to them.

Throughout her book there is a recognition of the importance of understanding Ancient Near Eastern culture. She presents an understanding of the long lives of antediluvian people, as recorded in Genesis 5, in terms of the ancient Mesopotamian numerological numbering system. [16 p48] The ancient Mesopotamians not only were accomplished mathematicians (They were using the Theory of Pythagoras a thousand years before Pythagoras was born.) but, in their sexagesimal arithmetic, they considered 60 to be sacred and its multiples to have special significance. She concludes *"that the patriarchal ages do not represent real numbers – they represent numerological numbers. Therefore, the genealogies of Genesis cannot be used for the construction of a chronology on an absolute time scale."* [16 p53] With this approach there is no conflict with the archaeological evidence from skeletons and clay tablets that life expectancy in these ancient times was more like 40 years than hundreds of years. [16 p48]

2 The idea of common descent for all living creatures proved difficult for some in the Church, but there were others who welcomed Darwin's ideas. David N. Livingstone wrote, *"There was no clear consensus as to what constituted the orthodox Calvinist line. Some, such as McCosh, Warfield and Strong, were willing supporters; others, such as A.A. Hodge, Patton and Shedd, remained tentative; others, including Dabney and Charles Hodge remained unconvinced, if not hostile."* [17 p130]

While some understood Darwinism to be founded on pure chance, denying purpose, and so denying a Creator, others kept an open mind recognising God's sovereignty even over chance events in the material order.

For B.B. Warfield (1851-1921), it was not a debate over Darwin's faith or lack of it. It was a debate about the idea that life could have evolved over long ages in the providence of God. On this he was clear that science had to settle the matter. Scripture did not pronounce on it. *"As far as Warfield was concerned it was possible to explain any given phenomenon in terms of either a religious cause or a scientific cause. This idea of 'concursus' was central to his theological project . . ."* [18 p117] Explanations in terms of natural causation

in no way negated a teleological explanation in terms of God's will. In this he claimed to be following the line taken by John Calvin. *"Calvin's ontology of second causes was, briefly stated, a very pure and complete doctrine of concursus, by virtue of which he ascribed all that comes to pass to God's purpose and directive government. What concerns us here is that he ascribed to second causes as their proximate account the entire series of modifications by which the primal indigested mass called heaven and earth has passed into the form of the ordered world which we see, including the origination of all forms of life, vegetable and animal alike, inclusive doubtless of the bodily form of man. And this, we say, is a very pure evolutionary scheme."* [19 p309]

BENJAMIN B. WARFIELD
1851 – 1921

On the antiquity of humans Warfield asserted, *"The question of the antiquity of man has of itself no theological significance . . . The Bible does not assign a brief span to human history; this is done only by a particular mode of interpreting the biblical data, which is found on examination to rest on no solid basis."* [19 p271]

At this point it is necessary to clarify three things. The first is that Warfield understood Calvin's doctrine of creation to say that in Genesis 1:1 we have God creating everything out of nothing. Subsequent verses describe a process of development until we come to the creation of humans which must also be creation from nothing. Warfield concludes from this that Calvin's doctrine of creation is *"for all except the souls of men, an evolutionary one."* [19 p308] Both he and Calvin strongly held the view that creation from nothing was a divine activity and that such creative actions occurred twice in the Genesis 1 narrative. Thus the first six days did not describe a series of creative acts, i.e. creation from nothing, but rather the development by the Creator of matter that he had brought into being from nothing in the beginning.

> "The Bible does not assign a brief span to human history."
>
> B. B. Warfield

It follows from this that they would not have been happy with some modern Christian views that see a multiplicity of creation acts down through the millennia to account for the variety of species we know today or even the existence of a bacterial flagellum. The material universe created in the beginning was pregnant with all that was necessary for the full flowering of the Creator's plan for the material universe.

Second, Warfield consistently held the view that evolution could never substitute for creation. Bringing matter into being, out of nothing, could never be achieved by evolution. God alone could achieve this. Likewise, God alone could make human beings in his own image. Evolution could only function as a theory describing the unfolding or development of matter but could never account for its origin. "*The quarrel of the Christian with evolutionism turns on the precise point that, not content with providing a schema for the method of creation, evolution substitutes itself for the fact of creation.*" [19 p189]

Third, Warfield remained convinced all this life that the theory of evolution had so far failed to muster the evidence necessary to establish it as a true picture of actual development of life on Earth. In 1895 he wrote, "*The only living question with regard to doctrine of evolution is whether it is true. And the only reasonable reply which can be given to this question today is that it is sub judice. This is not equivalent, of course, to saying it is not true. We may hold it to be probably true and yet agree that it is still upon its trial and has not yet been shown to be true.* [19 p165] B. B. Warfield died in 1922 before the full force of later developments in genetics have surfaced. In his younger days he had been interested in the breeding of cattle and would have been fascinated by later discoveries in genetics.

Warfield was a theologian who kept abreast of the scientific literature of his day. He firmly rejected all Darwinian speculation that denied purpose in creation and was not afraid to point to the lack of evidence for mechanisms that could provide the changes necessary to feed the process of natural selection. However, while he had a healthy scepticism of much of the current speculations surrounding Darwin's theory, he never concluded that the Bible in any way excluded the possibility of life evolving in the providence of God. Warfield wrote, "*I am free to say, for myself that I do not think that there is any general statement in the Bible, or any part of the account of creation, either as given in Gen. I and II, or elsewhere alluded to, that need be opposed to evolution. The upshot of the whole matter is that there is no necessary antagonism of Christianity to evolution."* [19 p130]

It is important to note that B.B. Warfield was the author of one of the most influential textbooks on Biblical authority, *The Inspiration and Authority of the Bible. "He was the most widely known advocate of confessional Calvinism in the United States at the end of the nineteenth and the beginning of the twentieth centuries."* [19 p16] Warfield was widely recognised as the champion

> "The upshot of it is that there is no necessary antagonism of Christianity to evolution."
>
> B. B. Warfield

of the doctrine of inspiration and a doughty warrior in defence of the Bible, during a time when liberal theologians were growing in influence.

Perhaps the idea of all animal life being descended from original single-celled organisms may be acceptable, but many become uneasy with the idea that the human species is part of that same *tree of life*? To the geneticist there is clear evidence of human physical descent from nonhuman species. To the theist it is of the utmost importance to see human beings as fundamentally distinct from all other animal species. Does this mean that the physical evidence and the Biblical evidence are at loggerheads? Not so. For the Bible, human beings are both material and spiritual. When we understand what it means to be truly human the tension disappears. The Creator sustains the universe in being according to his own plan and for his own purposes. These purposes could well have included the development of human-like species to the point where he would breathe into one or more of them to create something radically new, a human being made in his own image. John Stott called this new being, *"Homo Divinus."* This would indeed be an act of creation, producing something that is more than a development of existing life forms, something that is essentially new.

B.B. Warfield was prepared to allow for man's physical descent from pre-adamic species so long as it did not compromise either the teaching that the human being is created in the image of God, not a mere product of already created matter, nor compromise the essential unity of the human race. He was particularly adamant on this latter point as he stood firm against all forms of racism. *"The question of the unity of the human race differs from the question of its antiquity in that it is of indubitable theological importance . . . Outside of the influence of the biblical revelation, indeed, the sense of human unity has never been strong and has ordinarily been nonexistent."* [19 p279-280]

Today the evidence for descent with modification is undeniable. John Bryant states, *"Our biology, our genetics and the fossil evidence give every indication that we arrived here via evolution."* [20 p146] Indeed, the genetic code that is basic to all living organisms, including human beings, and the comparison of variations across the full range of living organisms puts this conclusion beyond reasonable doubt.

This raises important issues for our understanding of the creation of human beings. Who were Adam and Eve? What happened to Adam when he became a living being in a personal relationship with his Creator? How did Adam relate to the whole of humanity when God entered into a covenant relationship with him? Why did Adam's sin affect all human beings for all generations? These are important questions that must be thought through carefully. While the Biblical evidence is crucial in understanding humans as made in the image of God, scientific discovery can also help to steer us away from blind alleys in our journey to the truth.

3 Development of life through blind natural forces is probably the biggest issue for theists. This seems to imply physical determinism, deny any purpose and rule God out of the equation.

Random events occur in many areas of the natural world. Atoms of radioactive elements decay in an apparently random manner. It is impossible to predict which atom will decay next. Yet the half-life of a radioactive element is precise and unvarying. The time it takes for half the mass of a sample of radioactive material to decay is known and cannot be varied by any change in the circumstances of that sample. Air molecules move in apparent random fashion, the temperature of the air being a measure of the average speed of these molecules. This random movement is beautifully observed under the microscope in Brownian motion, the movement of the air molecules imparting random motion to small smoke particles. Yet the consequent temperature and pressure of the air can be precisely measured and obey the gas laws. Random events can lead to an ordered world.

Random mutations in the world of living things in no way denies purpose

Indeed, it is increasingly becoming apparent that the physical world has an element of randomness at its deepest levels of operation that seems to impart some kind of creativity, while upholding a material existence that is supremely ordered and mathematical in the macro world. The most fruitful field of scientific research in the last century lies in the area of Quantum Theory. There science learns to come to terms with probabilities rather than precision in the subatomic world, yet confident in the orderliness of the macro world.

Similarly, random mutations in the world of living things in no way denies purpose. It provides flexibility in adapting to stresses in the environment. Denis Alexander says, *"Of course, something that is 'pure chance' as far as we are concerned does not entail that it is 'pure chance' as far as God is concerned. If we take the concept of the immanence of God in the created order seriously, energised by the Spirit, existing in Christ, and providentially ruled by the Father, it is hard to know what ontological chance might mean from a heavenly perspective."* [21 p207]

Even within the natural world there is growing evidence that matter and energy seem to be so constituted as to have a bias in favour of life evolving. Simon Conway Morris, Emeritus Professor of Palaeobiology, University of Cambridge, says, *"there are hints that evolution has deeper organizational principles behind it, and may actually be quite an ordered process."* [4 p174] During a long and illustrious career he has pursued the concept of convergence in evolution. He says, *"Looking at the living world as a whole, it now seems as if evolutionary journeys are not a series of completely random or limitless wanderings but are following a network of well-worn paths."* [4 p99]

If there are laws guiding all that happens in both inanimate matter and in the living world does that not still leave the theist with a problem? Have we not simply swapped blind random forces for blind directive forces. In the past this fear was felt as heavenly bodies were found to obey the same inexorable laws of gravity as terrestrial bodies. If there is a scientific

Theism explains the origin of natural laws.

explanation for some phenomenon does that rule out a theological approach to the same phenomenon? Not so. The very orderliness of the world as seen through the eyes of science reinforces the idea of a wise Creator maintaining all in existence. Theism explains the origin of natural laws. Atheism simply has to accept their existence with no explanation for a world that is obstinately mathematical. To resolve this issue, we need to look at what we mean by natural laws.

God and the Laws of Nature

The laws of nature, as discovered through the scientific enterprise, are **descriptions** of what is observed in the material world. These descriptions are usually reduced to mathematical formulae, e.g. $e=mc^2$. They are not **prescriptions** as in commandments which must be obeyed. Much less are they some kind of force that can cause something to happen. They simply describe what exists. (In some popular presentations, 'Nature' or 'Evolution' are carelessly spoken of as if they were agents causing something to happen.)

So, why are there laws of nature and how does God fit into the picture? Among those who believe in a Creator there are a variety of beliefs with regard to His relationship to the created order.

At one end of the spectrum there are those who believe that the universe was brought into being by some divine watchmaker who, having made a watch, has no further interaction with it. God is seen as the one who created the heavens and the Earth and then had nothing more to do with it. They deny miracle and have no place for God incarnate. These are known as Deists. It is not hard to see how many modern agnostics and atheists were influenced by the writings of Deists.

> The laws of nature are descriptions of what is observed in the material world.

Others, known as Theists, believe God not only brought into being everything that exists (*"All things were made through him, and without him was not anything made that was made"* John 1:3), he himself being the only eternal self-existing being, they also believe that God continues to relate to what he has made. Without him nothing can continue to exist. *"In him all things hold together."* [Colossians 1:17] *". . . He sustains all things by his powerful word"* [Hebrews 1:3] The biblical view of the material world sees God in every event. *"Are not two sparrows sold for a penny? Yet not one of them will fall to the ground apart from your Father."* [Matthew 10:29] He is never absent from the world he created. God in creation and providence gives order to the physical world of matter and energy. This order is never independent of God. It is his thinking seen in action.

From our viewpoint, within our world, there is a natural order of events that makes science possible with its codifying of the laws of nature. From God's viewpoint, outside of our created universe, the very existence of material and spiritual entities and the unfolding of events are all his handiwork. The laws of nature simply describe **God's normal pattern of activity** as he sustains the cosmos in being. In this picture God does not intervene occasionally, like an absentee landlord, but is involved with all events at all times. However, we may talk of him intervening from time to time when he acts in such a way as to make it clear to his children that they are under his loving care and protection, e.g. a turn of events in answer to prayer. Having said all this it must be stressed that the Creator is not only always present but also separate from what he has made. The created order is not an extension of his being, but at the same time he is in constant contact with it.

Donald M. Mackay used the image of an author creating a story with all its complex characters, their world and all that happens to them. The unfolding universe is God's story in which we are his created characters. This, however, is different from the scenario of a three-dimensional human author creating a two-dimensional book with characters unable to make any meaningful decisions of their own. The divine author is so much greater than any human author and has populated his story with beings made in his own image, beings capable of thinking, loving and making responsible decisions. He even wrote himself into the story in the person of Jesus of Nazareth. We have this tension between divine sovereignty and human responsibility starkly stated by Peter in his Pentecost sermon where he talks of *"this man, handed over to you according to the definite plan and foreknowledge of God, you crucified and killed by the hands of those outside the law."* [Acts 2:23] How can this be? We don't know, any more than a two-dimensional being could understand the three-dimensional world except through the limited use of two-dimensional maps. God, who inhabits eternity, is so much greater than we can ever imagine.

In this view of the Creator and the creation, the 'laws of physics' include random events (in science these are events for which we do not know any determinant cause nor perceive any pattern) which sit happily with belief in purpose and design in nature. All events which, from the standpoint of the created realm arise from known causes or even from the action of an agent with free will, are, from the standpoint of the Creator his activity as he continuously upholds the universe. Even random events are not outwith his control. *"The lot is cast into the lap but the decision is the Lord's alone."* [Prov 16:33]

Where do miracles fit into this picture?

At the outset it is worth noting that it does no favours to God to see miracles as his tinkering with autonomous nature. Nature is not autonomous in the Biblical view and the laws of nature are thus not outwith the realm of God's sovereignty. When we resort to miracle to explain what we don't understand in the natural realm we end up with a 'god of the gaps', a god who is only needed to explain the things that appear inexplicable to us. The trouble with such explanations is that future generations find an acceptable natural cause for the events that puzzled us and so the progress in science leaves less and less room for such a god. Remember, the Biblical picture of God is of one who is sovereign and who works in an orderly manner.

We may find it useful to think of miracles in two categories (God's people in pre-scientific times would not have made such a distinction, simply being content with worshiping God for his amazing provision) – first, as breaks in the normal pattern of God's sustaining the material world, e.g. turning water into wine and Jesus' resurrection; second, as amazing timing of events, e.g. the parting of the Red Sea [Ex 14:21], where God caused an East wind to accomplish His purposes. Both of these scenarios fit perfectly into what has been described above. The miracles described in the Bible in no way contradict the scientific description of natural laws.

However, it is important to note that miracles are presented to us in Scripture as 'signs' and 'wonders' authenticating God's messengers and their message. They operate as signs because they break with the normal pattern. If there were no pattern then nothing could stand out as different. Miracles are tied in with redemptive revelation. They have a purpose. To resort to postulating miracle in order to explain the appearance of hundreds of thousands of new species throughout the billions of years of life on Earth may have the appearance of godliness but may also reduce God to the level of a defective workman who has to tinker with his creation to keep it going. It also devalues the very idea of miracle.

Scientists who are robustly theistic will always look for an explanation in terms of the normal order of the created world. They revel in the wonder of the order in Creation and are confident it has much to teach us yet.

Alec Motyer in a footnote (p30) to his commentary on Exodus (*The Bible Speaks Today*, BST) makes an interesting comment on the sovereignty of the Creator and his work of redemption. *"God's redemptive work is, therefore, not accurately seen in 'interventionist' terms. That is merely how it looks to the human observer. He is the ever-present, ever-active Creator [John 5:17], and his work in creation provides a basis for his work in redemption; his work in redemption fulfils his work in creation."*

Wonder and Awe

We started with James Clerk Maxwell thrilled by the mathematics of God's creation. Let us finish with a quick glance at the wonder and awe often experienced in the laboratory. The same sense of thinking God's thoughts after Him still motivates some scientist today. When they live their lives in obedience to God's calling and equipping, they discover much more than prosaic answers to the pointless riddles of the natural world.

Scientists are not robots. Their imagination and creativity form a significant part in directing their research. In a beautifully illustrated book, *Wonders of the Living World*, Ruth Bancewicz as editor allows eight scientists, working in diverse areas of 21st century science, to describe their work and the thrill it gives them.

Rhoda Hawkins, senior lecturer in physics, University of Sheffield, is one of them. She *"was drawn into science by her sense of wonder at the world, and her belief that it was made by someone good."* [4 p170] As a physicist she is researching the way living cells move and interact with other cells. She is intrigued when she sees randomness at one level resulting in order at a higher level. Randomly moving molecules stick together in the cell to form longer strands that build up a cytoskeleton that gives the cell its shape and inner organisation. She says, *"The more we find out about how living things work, the less 'mystery' there is – less of the ignorant or superstitious type of wonder. On the other hand, there is a greater sense of mystery, wonder, and excitement at the complexity of things: the beautifully coordinated mechanisms and clever solutions. There is also excitement at the questions that remain unanswered, and that is what drives science forward."* [4 p68]

As our scientific understanding of the functioning of living cells progresses we are constantly amazed by the wonder of the complexity and harmony of the whole process at molecular level. Let John Bryant point to just one remarkable process. *"Who would have thought that a turbine with moving parts could be made of protein, making it the smallest turbine on the planet. This protein is called ATP synthase and is actually composed of 18 different protein chains; so that there are in total, 29 protein chains in a single ATP synthase turbine in human cells . . . Each turbine . . . rotates at 120 revolutions per second, making three ATP molecules for each complete rotation . . . Overall, ATP synthase makes approximately our body's weight of ATP each day."* [20 p114] Using another marvel, this time of modern electronic technology, molecular animations of ATP synthase turbines can be viewed online. We are indeed *"fearfully and wonderfully made."* [Psalm 139:14]

Science in the laboratory helps bring to light the wonders of the living world and modern means of communications share that wonder with the wider world.

I hope this introduction to life evolving in the hands of God will help liberate us from human traditions that keep us back from appreciating the wonders of the created world, including the process of life evolving.

Conclusion

In this book I have argued for an approach to the Bible that sees it as God breathed, God's verbal revelation to humankind. I have pointed to scientific evidence for an ancient world in which life has evolved over long ages, evidence drawn from a variety of scientific disciplines yet forming a coherent picture. I have sought to demonstrate that from before the time of Darwin and during the early decades after the publication of "The Origin of Species", many Christians, especially from the Reformed presbyterian traditions, saw no clash between the idea of life evolving and Biblical teaching.

In an attempt to keep this book short, it is inevitable that there are many questions that will arise, demanding further reading. The short list of books on the final page is there to guide the reader into a deeper understanding of these topics. I have found my search for truth to be exciting and wish the reader much pleasure in their own journey of discovery in this fascinating area of truth.

For the avoidance of misunderstanding the following are my personal conclusions.

- The Scriptures of the Old and New Testaments are God's word, true in all they teach.
- God created from nothing all that exists and maintains it in existence.
- God's plan for creation will be fully realised in the new creation.
- Life has evolved over hundreds of millions of years from its simplest forms to the complex variety of life we know today.
- All life forms today, including human beings, are related through common physical descent.
- Adam was an historical character living at a time when there was already a population of Homo Sapiens with whom he shared the same DNA.
- Adam and Eve were created by God as material/spiritual beings in a personal relationship with himself.
- Adam was appointed by God to stand in relationship to the rest of humanity such that his disobedience affected all of humanity.
- What science uncovers resonates well with what the Bible teaches.
- The universe has been around for billions of years.
- There is purpose to our existence, discernible in both God's written word and in his creation.

I hope this summary of evidence and reasoning will bring some relief to those who have seen science, particularly evolution, as a threat. While some may not be convinced by the arguments laid out above, I hope we can move forward together in a reasoned debate and in a spirit of humility, "*speaking the truth in love*" [Eph. 4:15], always remembering that "*the wisdom from above is first pure, then peaceable, gentle, open to reason, full of mercy and good fruits, impartial and sincere.*" [James 3:17 (English Standard Version)]

Books I Found Helpful

1 Roger Wagner and Andrew Briggs, *The Penultimate Curiosity,* OUP, 2016

2 Francis Collins, *The Language of God*, Pocket Books, 2007

3 Alister McGrath, *Inventing the Universe*, Hodder, 2015

4 Ruth M. Bancewicz, *Wonders of the Living World*, Lion Hudson, 2021

5 Donald M. Mackay, *The Open Mind and other essays,* IVP, 1988

6 John H. Walton, *The Lost World of Genesis One*, IVP, 2009

7 John H. Walton, *The Lost World of Adam and Eve*, IVP, 2015

8 Gordon J. Wenham, *Word Biblical Commentary*, *Genesis 1-15*, Word Books, 1987

9 John Calvin, *A Commentary on Genesis*, Banner of Truth, English translation 1965

10 Melvin Tinker, *Reclaiming Genesis*, Monarch Books, 2010

11 Paul Marston, *Understanding the Biblical Creation Passages*, Lifesway, 2007

12 David Wilkinson, *The Bible Speaks Today - The Message of Creation*, IVP, 2002

13 Henri Blocher, *In the Beginning*, IVP, 1984

14 Alasdair Paine, *The First Chapters of Everything*, Christian Focus, 2014

15 Denis Alexander, *Creation or Evolution, do we have to choose?* Monarch 2008

16 Carol Hill, *A Worldview Approach to Science and Scripture*, Kregel Academic, 2019

17 David N. Livingstone, *Darwin's Forgotten Defenders*, Eerdmans, 1987

18 Gary L.W. Johnson (ed.), *B.B. Warfield, Essays on his Life and Thought*, P&R Publishing, 2007

19 Mark A. Noll and David N. Livingstone (eds.), *B.B. Warfield: Evolution, Scripture and Science selected writings*, Wipf and Stock, 2019

20 Graham Swinerd and John Bryant, *From the Big Bang to Biology: where is God?* Kindle Direct Publishing, 2020

21 Denis Alexander, *Is There Purpose in Biology?* Lion Hudson, 2018

Articles I found helpful

Meredith Kline, "Space and Time in the Genesis Cosmogony" An article which can be found at https://meredithkline.com/klines-works/articles-and-essays/

Tim Keller, "Creation, Evolution and Christian Laypeople" An article published online at: https://biologos.org/resources/scholarly-articles/creation-evolution-and-christian-laypeople

Websites I find invaluable

www.cis.org.uk
www.faraday-institute.org
www.biologos.org
www.thegodquestion.tv/explore